KU-033-890

Phillips

COLLECTORS GUIDES

ROCK & POP

Text ©   Alison Fox
Illustration ©   Phillips Fine Art
              Auctioneers
Edited by   Linda Doeser
Designed by   Strange Design Associates

Copyright © Dunestyle Publishing Ltd. and
Boxtree Ltd., 1988.

Boxtree Ltd.
36 Tavistock Street
London WC2 7PB

Conceived by Dunestyle Publishing Ltd.

All rights reserved. No part of this
publication may be reproduced, stored in a
retrieval system, or transmitted in any form
or by any means, electronic, mechanical or
otherwise, without prior permission in
writing of the copyright owners.

ISBN 1 85283 229 0

Typesetting by O'Reilly Clark, London
Colour separation by J Film Process Co Ltd.,
Bangkok, Thailand
Printed in Italy by New Interlitho spa.

Phillips
COLLECTORS GUIDES

ROCK & POP

ALISON FOX

BOXTREE

LONDON

Phillips, founded in 1796, has a reputation for specialisation. Its specialists handle fine art, antiques and collectors' items under more than 60 subject headings — a huge spectrum of art and artefacts that ranges from Old Masters and the finest antique furniture to cigarette cards and comparatively modern pop memorabilia. The auction group's Collectors' Centre, situated at Phillips West Two in Salem Road, Bayswater, London, is constantly recognising, defining and catering for new trends in collecting. It answers hundreds of queries a day from collectors, museums, dealers and the public at large. The shelves of its cataloguing halls are packed with a treasure-trove of objects, awaiting their turn to appear at auction. To varying extents, the scene there and in the main Mayfair salerooms (Phillips, 7 Blenheim Street, London W1Y 0AS; telephone 01-629 6602) is repeated at a score of Phillips branches elsewhere in Britain.

Contents

Introduction

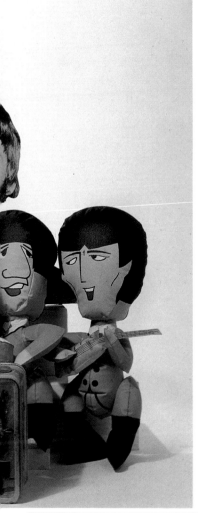

A collection of Beatles merchandise comprising cardboard coathangers made by Saunders Ent UK, inflatable Beatle caricatures made in Hong Kong, a Beatles lunchbox with flask and a very rare lampshade.

Rock and pop memorabilia has become the fastest growing field of collecting. The publicity that has surrounded the annual London auctions of rock and pop memorabilia has attracted a great many new enthusiasts. Although these auctions are comparatively recent, people have been collecting mementoes of music and stage stars since the late Victorian period when autograph collecting was in its heyday. However, it was only when the established auctioneers, Phillips, Christies and Sotheby's, began to include items of rock memorabilia in their sales that this area of collecting received a stamp of credibility and respectibility.

The first rock 'n' roll auction to take place in London was in 1981, when John Lennon's upright Steinway piano was offered for sale by auction. Its owners originally approached the Musical Instrument Department which, in a somewhat humiliating manner, passed it on to the Collectors Department which was known to be a little more adventurous. The piano created a great deal of publicity when it sold for £7,500/$12,000 and a flood of enquiries from the general public followed, as people discovered a mass of rock and pop memorabilia in their homes which, up to then, had either been forgotten about or was thought to be valueless. Since the first auction, the London salerooms have been holding annual and biannual sales specializing in rock 'n' roll and pop from the 1950s to the present day.

To begin with, the majority of items offered for sale were related to The Beatles and Elvis Presley but, as these items fetched such high prices, many collectors started to look round for mementoes of other artists.

A film poster for Play It Cool starring Billy Fury, Helen Shapiro and Bobby Vee.

Gradually, over the years, the number of items appearing for sale associated with The Rolling Stones, The Who and other 1960s and 70s artists has grown. Memorabilia of stars of the 1950s, including Gene Vincent, Buddy Holly, Bill Haley, Eddie Cochran, Lonnie Donegan and the young Elvis, is rare and at a premium. A gold disc presented to Gene Vincent for his song 'Be-Bop-A-Lula' sold for £9,000/$14,400 in 1987, and a single song sheet for Buddy Holly and The Crickets 'That'll Be The Day' sold for £90/$144 in 1988.

The number of Beatles' fans and collectors in the late 1980s has become quite a phenomenon. There are monthly magazines, books, conventions, fan clubs, newsletters and fairs totally devoted to the collector of Beatles' memorabilia. At the end of August each year, a Beatles' Convention takes place in Liverpool, when collectors of Beatles' memorabilia meet up. There are film and video shows, exhibitions, and a fair where collectors can buy from the new and growing breed of Beatles' dealers. To coincide with the Liverpool convention, all the major auction rooms in London and one in Liverpool gather together collections of rock and pop memorabilia and each holds a sale during the week. It is now known as 'Beatles' week and it attracts many American, Japanese and Scandinavian collectors to England.

Items associated with John Lennon are likely to be in greater demand than those related to the other three Beatles, probably because he is dead. It is sad but true that when any successful artist dies, he immediately becomes more collectable, and there is great demand for memorabilia of John Lennon, Jimi Hendrix, Keith Moon, Brian Jones, Jim Morrison, Marc Bolan and Elvis Presley.

As the number of rock and pop memorabilia collectors grows, so the prices increase. Many collectors can no longer afford to buy memorabilia relating to Buddy Holly, The Beatles and Elvis Presley, and items associated with The Rolling Stones and The Who are already catching up. Collectors are now looking at the lesser stars of the 1950s and 60s and the more recent performers of the 1970s and 80s. An artist need not have died nor need a band be from an earlier period to be collectable. The pop stars of the 1980s can be just as collectable, depending on how popular they are, how long the band stayed together and their public profile. If a contemporary artist often refuses to sign his autograph, an example could well be worth more than one of a more famous 1960s star who always obliged. The most collectable artists from the 1980s are Boy George, Michael Jackson, Madonna, Prince, Phil Collins, Paul McCartney, Dire Straits, Bob Geldof, The Police, U2, Brian Ferry and Queen.

In the late 1980s, three new fields of collecting within the field of rock and pop have emerged — psychedelia, New Wave and R &

B. Following the 20th anniversary of the release of the legendary Sargeant Pepper album, many television films and documentaries were repeated and a number of features on the year of 1967 appeared in magazines and newspapers. At about the same time, a number of wildly decorated silk screen posters — forgotten for 20 years — started to appear in the salerooms. The new wave or punk movement of the late 1970s produced a radical new style of music and design. Groups, including the Sex Pistols, The Damned, Generation X and The Cure, enjoyed a short lived success, and early recordings of their music, artwork for their albums, posters and promotional items are now very collectable. A contract for the last professional English appearance of the Sex Pistols in 1977 sold for £300/$480 in 1986. In 1988, a single promotional Sex Pistols tour poster was fetching between £200-£300/$320-$480.

One of the most appealing aspects of collecting rock and pop memorabilia is the range of items to choose from. There is a multitude of records — released, early promotional copies and acetates, novelty records and gold discs. There are autographs, letters, contracts and manuscript material, tour programmes,

Beatles memorabilia comprising Beatles 'Strange Masks', Washington Pottery cup and saucer, Christmas flexi discs and a fan club card.

posters, tour jackets, tickets and T-shirts. There are personal articles of clothing, furniture, cars and art, photographs, postcards, novelty toys, fan club booklets and musical instruments. Whether you have £1/$3.20 to spend on a record, £10/$16 to spend on a set of Beatles' cake decorations, £50/$80 to spend on an original Siouxsie and The Banshees' tour poster, £500/$800 to spend on an album signed by the Sex Pistols, or £3,000/$4,800 to spend on a stage suit that originally belonged to John Lennon, there is something for every collector.

The question, who are the people to buy from these specialized auction of rock and pop memorabilia, is often asked. The collectors of Beatles' memorabilia are often dedicated fans from the 1960s. Their whole lives might revolve around The Beatles: letterheads carry pictures of The Fab Four, and they collect all newspaper cuttings, magazine articles, fan club newsletters and auction catalogues. They own every book ever written on The Beatles, every released record and attend every Beatles' convention. They often have limited means, but attend every auction and viewing prior to the sale to see close at hand items they can only dream of owning.

The auctions have lent an air of respectability to collecting rock and pop related articles, and some mature rock and pop connoisseurs have started private collections of high-quality material, many with a view to investment. A number of American collectors, who have been connected with the music business in some way, have a good background knowledge of the items now being offered for sale. Many are successful

Below A collection of magazines relating to Elvis Presley and The Beatles.

businessmen who can afford to spend large sums of money on a good John Lennon drawing, autograph or guitar. They study each auction catalogue and the prices obtained are stored on their computers, so, at a glance, they know how much they should spend on an item and how much their own collections are appreciating in value. They might not have time to attend the sales, but often bid by telephone during the auction.

Museums are becoming more interested as the market matures. Jimmy Velvet's Elvis Presley Museum in Nashville has a mass of memorabilia which Jimmy has been collecting privately and from the major auction rooms over a period of 20 years. The Theatre Museum in London, situated at the old flower market in Covent Garden, has a growing collection of pop memorabilia on display, including Beatles' stage suits and dazzling stage costumes belonging to The Jackson Five. Madame Tussauds, the famous

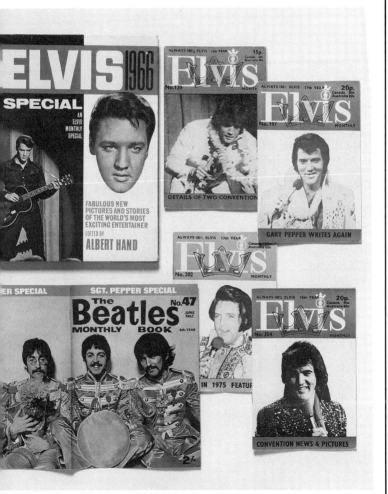

London waxworks, also buys items of personal clothing for its exhibition of waxwork pop idols.

An auction of rock and pop in London or New York in the 1980s would not be the same without the presence of someone representing The Hard Rock Café chain. The Hard Rock owns restaurants in London, New York, Dallas, Tokyo, Los Angeles, Honolulu and Sydney. It has the world's largest collection of rock and pop memorabilia, most of it displayed on the walls of its different restaurants. For enthusiastic rock collectors, a tour of each is essential and a printed guide is available to each diner. In words taken from the guide, The Hard Rock Café is a 'self motivating, non nuclear powered memorabilia tour of the world's only rock and roll museum'. Among the items on show in the London restaurant are Bill Wyman's Framus bass guitar, Jimi Hendrix's silver stage belt, Marc

Bolan's original handwritten lyrics for 'Metal Guru', the original telegram sent to Brian Epstein from Colonel Tom Parker welcoming The Beatles to the US, Little Richard's snakeskin stage boots, David Bowie's signed 501 jeans, and John Lennon's velvet-lapelled jacket. With the Hard Rock Café buying a number of the rarer items of rock and pop interest, many collectors have become disilllusioned and frequently complain that, if the

Hard Rock want to buy something, it will outbid everyone else. This has been true of some items, but for the many collectors and fans who cannot afford to pay more than £50/$80 for an item, The Hard Rock Café offers an opportunity to view these historic items in a public display; otherwise, they might be hidden away in some private collector's home in America or Japan.

With many different collectors bidding at sales, forcing the price

Two rare items from the Apple Corporation — the Apple Watch, which, in original box, can sell for £200/$320 and The Apple Dartboard, given by the Beatles to friends and employees. In 1987 one sold at auction for £720/$1,152.

BRYAN FERRY

"Don't Stop the Dance"

7" and 12"

of important memorabilia to go sky high, the press and media have a field day. Often at the London auctions there are film crews from America, Europe and Japan. The publicity that follows these sales has, by and large, a good effect, bringing many undiscovered items on to the market.

A limited edition promotional poster for Bryan Ferry's 'Don't Stop the Dance' record signed by Ferry.

The assistant photographer, who worked with Michael Cooper on the set for the Sgt. Pepper album cover, contacted Phillips in 1987 to ask whether some of the old cardboard cut-outs from the set would be of interest. When they were delivered, they turned out to be the original life-size, blow-up cut-outs designed by Peter Blake and representing Merkin, Dion, Oliver Hardy, Marilyn Monroe, Shirley Temple, Stan Laurel, Carl Jung, and a garden gnome signed by all four members of The Beatles. In the Phillips sale in August 1987, the gnome sold for £5,500/$8,800 and the cut-outs totalled £11,000/$17,600.

One of the bad effects of all this publicity is that many people believe that anything and everything to do with The Beatles is worth a small fortune and they are disappointed when their set of Beatles' autographs sells for £250/$400, compared with a John Lennon handwritten manuscript selling for £11,000/$17,600. As with all spheres of collecting, the uninitiated find it difficult to differentiate between good and poor quality.

For new collectors, there are three basic questions. What to buy? Where to buy? and How much to pay? What to buy depends on each individual collector. He might choose to compile a cross-section of memorabilia of just one artist, or choose to focus on one field of collecting, for example, records or autographs. The amount of storage space available will also determine the type of memorabilia he can collect. Not everyone has the room to store jukeboxes and drum kits. Once a collector has decided which path to take, whether it be bubblegum cards, records or autographs, his ultimate aim is to compile a complete collection.

There are many places to find memorabilia. The most publicized settings are the London and New York auction houses. The enormous media coverage that these sales attract means that the auction houses are inundated with inquiries and property. The specialists in charge of these sales see a huge number of items each week, only a quarter of which is probably worth taking in for sale. Phillips, Christies and Sotheby's produce catalogues for their sales, published approximately three weeks before the sale. An annual catalogue subscription will ensure that no sales are missed.

There is always a viewing day before the sale, when prospective buyers can examine the lots that might interest them. If a collector cannot attend an auction, he can leave bids by telephone or post. A few overseas collectors prefer to bid live by telephone. One facility which few collectors seem to make use of is to ask for a condition report before leaving a telephone or postal bid. The specialists are happy to check the quality and condition of an item for any prospective buyer.

If a collector examines a copy of *Record Collector* in the UK or *Goldmine* in the USA, he will note that a large number of record fairs take place around the country each month. These fairs provide a useful meeting place for collectors, who can share

John Lennon's handwritten lyrics for 'Jealous Guy'. Sold in 1988 for £4,200/$6,720.

A Washington pottery Beatles' mug.

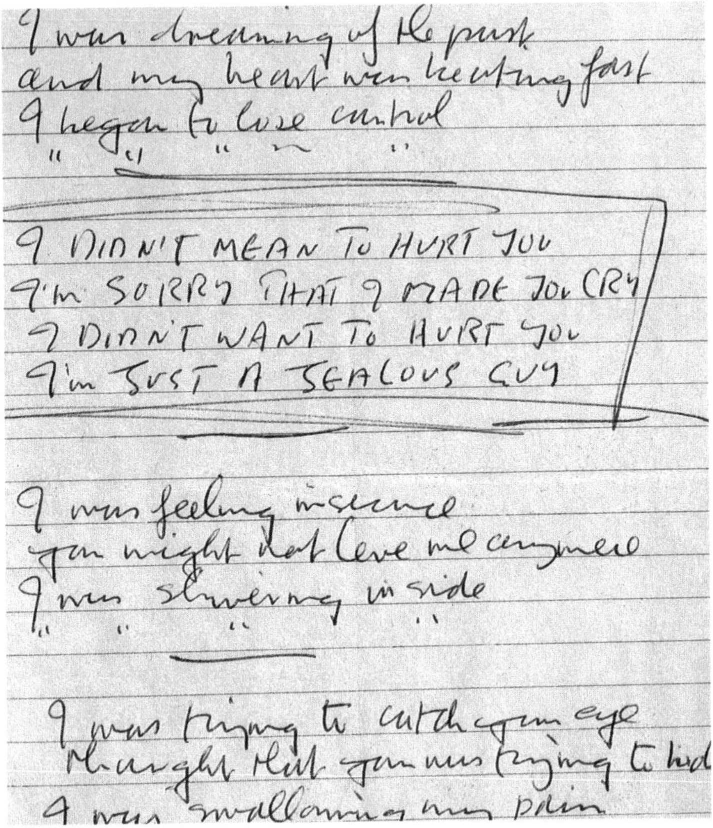

I was dreaming of the past
and my heart was beating fast
I began to lose control
"   "   "   "   "

I DIDN'T MEAN TO HURT YOU
I'M SORRY THAT I MADE YOU CRY
I DIDN'T WANT TO HURT YOU
I'm JUST A JEALOUS GUY

I was feeling insecure
you might not love me anymore
I was shivering inside
"   "   "   "   "

I was trying to catch your eye
Thought that you was trying to hide
I was swallowing my pain

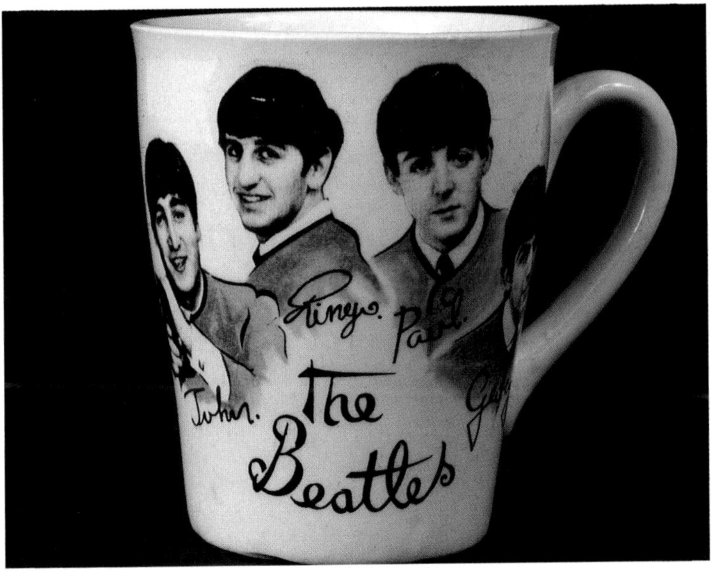

information on the state of the market and any counterfeits that might be circulating. They are also good places to buy and sell. Dealers at these fairs are not always scrupulous, so be cautious when buying. It is always wise to ask for a letter of authenticity to accompany your purchase.

It is surprising how many items of memorabilia are still being discovered at jumble sales, garage sales and bric a brac stalls. A number of Beatles

usherette style dresses have been found from these sources, together with Beatles' ties, tablecloths and pottery. Tour programmes, tickets, magazines, newspapers, books and board games can be found in second-hand book shops.

Record Collector magazine offers a comprehensive guide to collectors of records and memorabilia. Each month, the magazine publishes a complete discography, profiles a band, lists

fairs and conventions and writes auction reviews. It also contains a large classified advertisement section at the rear where collectors and dealers advertise their wants and items for sale.

What should a collector pay? In such a new area of collecting, prices can be very speculative. Auction estimates are based on the most recent sale price for a similar item, but if an article has not come up for auction before, it can be anybody's guess as to its worth. When a rare object is offered for sale at auction, often even the specialist has no idea what it may fetch. Auctions can be volatile. When an item sells for a high price, it may be because it is rare; it may also be because two collectors both badly need it for their collections. The next year, if a similar item comes up for auction with one fewer collector bidding, it may go for a great deal less. Items, particularly records and novelty items, may also vary

Eight of the tinted photographic enlargements used on the set of the cover photograph for the album Sgt Pepper's Lonely Hearts Club Band comprising from left to right Carl Jung, Merkin, Dion, Marilyn Monroe, Oliver Hardy, Stan Laurel, the garden gnome and Shirley Temple. The collection totalled £11,000/$17,600 in 1987.

in value from country to country. Autographs are more readily available in the UK and American collectors and dealers often buy them to sell at a profit in America. What a collector ultimately pays for a piece of memorabilia is based on how important he believes it is to his collection. The Rolling Stones' fan who purchased the earliest known acetate bearing their 1962 recording 'Close Together' and 'You Can't Judge A Book' for £6,000/$9,600, was rumoured to have taken out a second mortgage on his home!

Most memorabilia of famous artists purchased in the early 1980s has proved to be a worthwhile investment. However, now and again, a high-priced piece will start to fall in value when the publicity has brought a number of similar items on to the market. The original die-cast Corgi toy Yellow Submarine in its original box was fetching over £200/$320 in 1985, but it was selling for just £90/$144 in 1987 as

Below A sculpture by John Somerville of John Lennon *c.* 1985. A limited edition of 30/50.

Far right Max and the Head Blue Meanie celluloid from The Beatles' film A Yellow Submarine

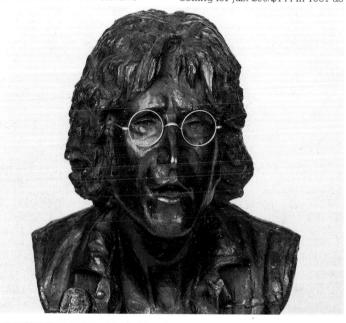

rumours spread that 500 identical boxed sets had been found in a warehouse. A complete set of *Beatles Book Monthly* magazines, 77 in the set and issued between 1963 and 1969, would cost a collector £500/$800 in 1985 but the following year, after a flood of sets appeared, they were selling for as little as £132/$220. In 1988, a complete set was fetching £300/$480 which is a good indication of how volatile the market can be.

One of the pitfalls of this new collecting surge is the number of unscrupulous dealers who take advantage of the inexperienced collector. Fake and reproduction items have been produced in the most unexpected fields. In each of the following chapters I have attempted to make collectors buy with a degree of caution. The best advice I can give is to examine the source of the memorabilia in detail and, when buying an object, ask for a letter of authenticity from the vendor.

Even the most experienced collector will admit to having been caught out at least once in the past.

Many artists have been astonished at the interest their memorabilia has been arousing in the auction rooms. Record companies, quick not to miss a trick, are now producing limited edition books, records and posters which become collectable on publication. Both Paul McCartney and George Harrison have produced leather-bound collectors' edition books. At the Phillips charity sale in spring 1987, a number of limited edition items were donated by record companies and artists. A pizza-style boxed set of cassette, record and compact disc of their Joshua Tree recording was donated by U2. One of only 300 produced, the pizza-box was fetching £200/$320 on release. Brian Ferry donated two stylish limited edition posters, each signed for 'Slave to Love' and

'Windswept'. They sold for £420/$672 and £300/$480 respectively. Picture discs are also being produced in limited editions.

What is there in the future? Over the last eight years, collecting rock and pop memorabilia has gone from strength to strength. It is difficult to judge who of the late 1980s artists will be the most collectable in the future. My guess would be Michael Jackson, Prince, Madonna, The Beastie Boys and Bruce Springsteen. Any item of quality, including records, limited edition books, posters or records, tour jackets, personal clothing, guitars and other instruments are always a wise investment. In 1988, there were many novelty items available in stores. A collector could choose from a Boy George hat or hologram, Beastie Boys hats, calendars and badges, (if all the VW logos have already been stolen from the cars in your road), Pepsie and Shirlie skirts, Madonna sunglasses, Michael Jackson bendy dolls and Rolling Stones telephones, plus a cart load of ephemeral items which may well become collectable in the future.

Lifesize cutouts of The Beatles as they appear in the film 'Yellow Submarine'. These figures stood in the foyer of the Pavilion Theatre for the premiere of the film and sold for £1,300/$2,080 in 1988.

Chapter One

A RECORD OF POP

Three rare types of records, a demonstration record, a triangular centre record and an acetate.

Record collecting is fun and affordable and records are easy to find. There are also numerous ways in which to specialize. Most collectors begin by choosing their favourite artist, others choose an era or a type of music, like Rhythm and Blues, Skiffle, Rock 'n Roll or Punk.

There are many places to find records for your collection. Most large towns in Europe and America have specialist shops dealing in old record releases, many of which are run by people who have been connected with the music industry and whose knowledge is extensive. Record fairs are held regularly and are advertised in record collecting magazines. It is essential to attend these fairs to meet dealers and collectors, check market prices and to buy and sell your records. Much collecting is done by word of mouth. The major auction rooms are also beginning to include more records in specialized rock and pop auctions and advertise these sales in the press. Catalogues can be ordered by subscription.

The greatest help to the new collector are the specialist record magazines, *Record Collector* magazine in the UK and *Goldmine* in the USA are available by subscription and from newsagents. *Record Collector* is published monthly and each issue profiles a band and details a complete discography of its work. The magazine also gives details of special pressings, foreign releases and limited edition, collectors' items, accompanied by an up-to-date market price guide. Near the end of the magazine are pages where collectors place advertisements for records they wish to sell or obtain. It is therefore easy for a collector to compile a comprehensive guide to all the releases he might wish to collect.

There are different types of records to collect. The classic 78s of the legendary Buddy Holly, Elvis Presley and Bill Haley and the Comets are very collectable and fetch between £5/$8 and £15/$24 a copy, but the majority of 78s are almost impossible to sell. They are made of a brittle plastic and they tend to crack and scratch easily. Auctions can include large lots of 78s but they must be in excellent condition. A lot at a Phillips' auction in 1988, comprising over 450 78 rpm records including artists Perry Como, Lonnie Donnegan and Pat Boone, all in excellent condition, sold for only £120/$192, whereas a very rare 78 rpm record by Elvis Presley, entitled 'That's Alright Mama/Blue Moon of Kentucky', on the Sun Label and made as early as 1954, sold in 1988 for £200/320. Another of his records entitled 'Milkcow Blues/You're a Heartbreaker' recorded in 1955 on the Sun label, sold for

£140/$224 at the same auction.

In the 1950s, 45 rpm records were introduced but it was not until 10 years later that they became very popular. The early 45s are, therefore, very rare. The song 'That's Alright Mama/Blue Moon of Kentucky', recorded on a 45 rpm by Elvis Presley fetched £300/$480 at auction in 1988. Extended plays, commonly known as EPs, bridging the gap between the single and long playing record, became popular in the 1960s. EPs usually feature four or five tracks by an artist and come in colourful picture sleeves. When buying EPs, always check that the original is inside the cover, not a re-release placed there by an unscrupulous dealer.

Long-playing records, commonly called LPs, became very popular in the late 1960s. Many artists, including Led Zeppelin, relied totally on the LP, never having released a single commercially. It is advisable when buying an LP to check whether it has been recorded in

Seven Beatles Christmas flexi-discs

mono or stereo. The Beatles' first LP 'Please Please Me' was recorded in 1963 in both mono and stereo. The stereo copy bearing a gold/black label is now fetching five times that of the mono edition on the same colour label.

Novelty records, which include flexi-discs, are sought after by many collectors. The most popular are the flexi-discs produced by the Official Beatles' Fan Club as a Christmas gift to their fans in the years between 1963 and 1969. These thin, bendy, plastic records were fetching £25-£50/$40-$80 each in the mid-1980's.

Many collectors are happy to stop collecting once they have managed to obtain all the commercial releases and move on to another artist or era. However, many adventurous collectors move on to collect the unreleased recordings, known as acetates, demos and promos.

An acetate is a metal disc

Below Elvis Presley's rarest records. 45rpm and 78rpm versions of his first recording 'That's Alright Mama' on the Sun record label *c.* 1954.

Far right A Dick James acetate for the Beatles song. 'This Boy' *c.* 1963.

covered in black vinyl, usually only recorded on one side, bearing a white label often with a handwritten or typed song title and other recording details, including a date. An acetate is made early in the recording of a song to give the producer an idea of the sound and for the band to hear how its sound is progressing. Sometimes only one or two acetates are made and, as they often differ from the final release, they are very collectable and can fetch very high prices. One of the most exciting acetates to appear at auction in recent years was recorded by The Rolling Stones in 1962, with Tony Chapman as drummer. It is believed to be the first recording made by The Rolling Stones. The acetate bore three tracks 'Soon Forgotten', 'Close Together' and 'You Can't Judge a Book' and was recorded on an Emidisc label.

Record Collector, reviewing this particular record in April 1988, added 'The acetate is liberally covered with scratches and hiss which makes the fledgling Stones sound rather more like The Jesus and Mary chain. But as it is the only record of the pre-Watts/Wyman Rolling Stones, it is still a fascinating historical document. It is remarkable that it has remained undiscovered for all these years and shows that in the world of record collecting, there always is the chance that your next visit to a junk shop or second-hand store might just turn up an item of unimaginable value. The value to historians is incalculable.' On 6th April, 1988, at a Phillips sale of rock and pop memorabilia, the acetate sold to a dedicated Rolling Stones fan for £6,000/ $9,600. In the same sale, a two-sided 12-inch acetate for The Rolling Stones song 'Get Your Ya Ya's Out!' sold for £520/$832.

Demonstration, promotional and disc jockey records were produced by record companies in limited numbers to be sent to

journalists and DJs before the release of a record. As they were recorded fairly early, they can sometimes differ from the eventual release and are, therefore, of great interest to collectors. The 1960s promos and demos are easily identifiable for their labels differ from the commercial release. The label can often vary in colour and is usually marked with the printed words 'Promo release — Not for Sale' or 'for demonstration purposes only'. Many bear a large 'A' across the label. Prices for demos and promos vary according to the popularity of the artist. If the artist does not have a following, a demonstration record will sell for little more than the commercial release. A Beatles demonstration record on a Dick James Music Ltd. label for the song 'This Boy' sold for £180/$288 in 1988. A Rolling Stones promo on the Decca label was fetching between £30/$48 and £40/$72 in the mid-1980s, whilst Davie Jones (alias David Bowie) and The King Bees' promos on Parlophone label can fetch upwards of £100/$160.

It is advisable for all collectors to obtain as much information as possible on counterfeit and bootleg records. By keeping in touch with the record magazines, talking to collectors and dealers at record fairs and auctions, a collector will soon learn of any doubtful records circulating. The rarest records are most likely to be fake. Elvis Presley's record 'TV Guide Presents Elvis Presley' is so rare that it has a market value of £4,000/$6,400 and there are countless counterfeit copies available. Another Elvis Presley record that has been counterfeited is an LP entitled 'Janis and Elvis' on the RCA label. This rare 10-inch record was pressed in South Africa by Teal

Record Co. and in 1988 the original was fetching over £800/$1,280.

It is possible to identify a counterfeit record by its label. Many counterfeit labels differ in colour from the original, the printed details are often blurred or a different size. To a well-trained eye, thickness, weight or surface of the record itself might seem wrong.

The term bootleg is used for any recording which has been sold or transported illegally. A bootleg could be a concert recording or an unreleased studio session. The quality of the sound is often poor and the vinyl cheap. Any one caught bootlegging material is breaking the law and if caught, can face criminal charges. You have been warned!

When buying records, collectors must always check the condition of the disc. There is a recognized grading system of condition used by magazines and often by auction rooms. The system begins with Mint — records that have never been played; Excellent — records played only a couple of times; Very good — records that have a few surface scratches which do not detract from the recording; down to the lowest grade, Poor. Few collectors will consider buying records below the Very good grade unless the record is particularly rare, when condition is secondary to the rarity of the release.

It is not only the condition of the vinyl that is important. Often collectors are discouraged from buying a record if it lacks its centre. The early triagular centres released in the late 1950s are often found to be missing. If a record label has been scribbled over or torn, it will also detract from its desirability. I was one of

Below The Rolling Stones first known recording on an EMI disc 7" acetate sold for £6,000/$9,600 in 1988.

Bottom A white label HMV demonstration record for Elvis Presley's song 'Blue Suede Shoes'.

many who proudly wrote my name on the record label not knowing that one day this would cause frustration to collectors.

Careful storage is important. Records should be stored upright and not too close together, as this can cause them to warp. They should be protected by a cardboard cover. Each collector seems to have his own preference about cleaning his collection. A variety of materials, from soap and water, alcohol, washing up liquid and liquid soap, have been used. It is best to experiment until you find a method that suits you.

Chapter Two

SIGN LANGUAGE

The collecting of autographs has been an established hobby since Queen Victoria's reign. By 1988, there were over 60,000 worldwide collectors belonging to the Universal Autograph Collectors' Club (the UACC).

What is an autograph? It is rather neatly explained by this anecdote, courtesy of writer Peter Johnson. 'The late Ray Rawlins, a British collector of autographs and documents asked the then Duke of Devonshire for his autograph, the Duke wrote in his proffered book; "You are a nuisance". Rawlins reminded the Duke that he had failed to sign it whereupon the Duke appended "Devonshire" remarking that he had been asked for his autograph rather than his signature. Rawlins realized that Devonshire was drawing the distinction between autograph and signature and henceforth never forgot the golden rule that every signature is an autograph but not every autograph is a signature.'

In the 1980s, the auctions of rock memorabilia have regularly included autographs from the 1950s through to the 1980s. It is sad but true that whenever a pop star dies, his signature becomes much more collectable. Autographs of John Lennon, Jimi Hendrix, Jim Morrison, Marc Bolan, Elvis Presley, Brian Jones and Sid Vicious are all very sought-after and now fetching high prices.

Autographs vary greatly in quality and this is reflected in their value. A plain and scruffy piece of paper bearing a set of the Beatles' signatures will fetch £100/$160 compared to an original manuscript by John Lennon which can fetch upwards of £10,000/$16,000. It is, however, still possible in the late 1980s to find autographs of 1960s artists for under £25/$40.

Quality and condition are most important. The autograph must be clear, preferably in ink, and the material it is written on in good condition. Many fans waiting outside stage doors in the 1960s would, in their eagerness, tear out a page from their small autograph books for their idol to sign and, when they returned home, would stick it back in the book with tape. Twenty years on, the tape has yellowed and become unsightly. Some fans, in their innocence, even taped over the signatures in a misguided attempt to preserve their treasured finds.

One of the best ways of buying autographs is to keep an eye out for these small autograph books. They often appear at auction and can include a multitude of 1960s artists, including The Beatles, The Rolling Stones, The Who, The Kinks, Donovan, Cliff Richard and

Below The Sex Pistols 'Never Mind The Bollocks' LP cover signed by all the band on the front cover. Sold for £550/$880 in 1988.

Bottom The Beatles first American LP 'Introducing The Beatles' signed and dedicated by all four Beatles *c.*1963. Sold for £1,100/$1,600 in 1988.

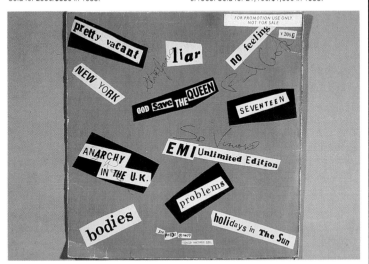

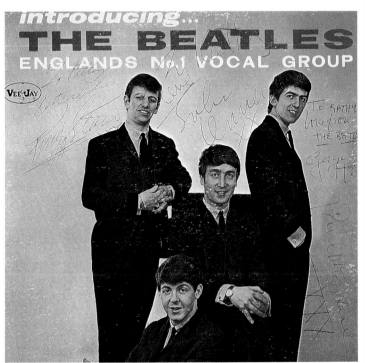

others. In the mid-1980s books of this nature can be bought for approximately £200/$320 at auction. Often collectors are just after one signature in the book and will take this out and then re-enter the book in a subsequent auction.

Signed records are very sought-after. They may be signed by each member of the group on the record label or, more commonly, on the front or back of the LP or EP cover. Good signed albums, in particular those signed by The Beatles, are an excellent investment, with prices soaring in the late 1980s. A Vee Jay American album for The Beatles entitled 'Introducing The Beatles', signed in blue pen by all four on the front cover during The Beatles first US tour, fetched an unbelievable figure of £1,000/$1,600 at a Phillips auction in 1988. At the same sale The Beatles 'Please, Please Me' album signed in blue ink on the front and originally donated by The Beatles to a charity fête fetched £550/$880. A signed copy of The Beatles' first single, 'Love Me Do' (1962), signed by all four on one side of the label after a concert at Earleston Town Hall in November 1962, sold to a Japanese collector at a London auction room for £850/$1,360.

It is not only records signed by The Beatles that are fetching high prices. In 1988, at the Phillips Spring sale, material signed by various artists soared. A Rolling Stones album (c. 1964), signed by the band, including Brian Jones, fetched £160/$256. A Michael Jackson 'Off the Wall' album, signed on the front, fetched £150/$240. Bob Dylan's album 'Real Live', signed by him on the front in silver pen, fetched £60/$96, but the biggest surprise of all was The Sex Pistols' 'Never

Mind the Bollocks' LP, signed by all the band, including Sid Vicious and Johnny Rotten, which sold for £520/$832. The more popular the artist and the rarer the record, the higher the value. In general, albums signed on the front are more desirable as many collectors wish to frame and display them.

With display in mind, collectors also favour signed photographs. The rarer the photograph signed, the more collectable it is. A signed publicity photograph of Elvis Presley, in very good condition, sold for £200/$320 in 1988 and a small, scruffy, torn photograph of Elvis Presley shaking hands with a fan in the backyard of the house he rented in Germany during his army days fetched £260/$416. The photograph was in poor condition and the signature was rubbed, but it was rare and unpublished. The Official Beatles' Fan Club cards that were sent out to fans are often signed and are always popular with collectors, in particular, in America. Collectors have been known to buy them in London for £200-£300/$320-$480 and resell for £600/$960 on their return to the United States.

Original programmes signed by the artist following a concert or reception on tour are becoming increasingly collectable. Some appear at auction and the rarer the concert, the more in demand the programme will be. A concert programme for The Beatles' mini-tour of Scotland in 1963, when they visited Glasgow, Kirkcaldy and Dundee, signed by the four on the front fetched £700/$1,120 at auction in 1988, and a 1964 tour programme sold for £500/$800 a year earlier. A rare Australian tour programme for The Rolling Stones' tour of 1966, signed on the front cover for a determined 12-year-old girl

A publicity photograph of Bill Haley and His Comets, signed by each member.

BILL HALEY And His COMETS
Decca Recording Artists

Personal Direction
Jas. H. FERGUSON
801 Barclay Street
Chester, Pa. 2-3004

Exclusive Booking
JOLLY JOYCE
1619 Broadway, New York City
Room 716   PLaza 7-1786
Philadelphia: WAlnut 2-4677—2-3172

during a plane flight, recently sold for £220/$320.

Signed books are very popular with all rock memorabilia collectors. The two commonest books to appear at auction are John Lennon's *In His Own Write* and *A Spaniard in the Works*. These books signed by John Lennon on the fly leaf have been fetching a steady £200-£300/$320-$480 in the mid-1980s. When the books contain a message, an amusing dedication or one of John's famous doodles, they can be worth a great deal more. Dr Walter Strach, business adviser to The Beatles and literary agent for *A Spaniard in the Works* recently sold his own copy through Phillips. The book bore the inscription 'To Walter, please make me richer than you John Lennon (a pal)'. This copy sold to a delighted collector in America for £650/$1,040. Another copy of *A Spaniard in the Works*, signed and dedicated by John Lennon 'To "Thingis" Photo News from "Thingy", sold, in 1985, for £500/$800. George Harrison produced a leather-bound collectors' edition of his book *I Me Mine*, signed and numbered, and in the mid-1980s it was selling for over £400/$640.

The more unusual the item signed, the more eager collectors are to acquire it. A cheque from John Lennon to the Inland Revenue for the sum of £6,966.10.0d, (£6,966.50/$11,146.40) signed in black ink and dated 23 January, 1968, sold for £4,800/$7,680 in a Phillips auction in 1988. The buyer, who was in the process of fighting a £60,000/$96,000 tax demand, bought the cheque because it was made out to the Inland Revenue. She told me 'I would have paid whatever it took to get it. It's a light-hearted protest against the taxman.' The

Below A Beatles cotton usherette dress worn at the premiere of the film 'A Hard Day's Night', and signed by The Beatles at the neck.

cheque had been estimated at £400–£600/$640–$960. A pair of Michael Jackson's dance shoes, both signed by him, sold in the same auction for £3,800/$6,080. A pink and white polka dot dress, one of eight worn by the usherettes for the Royal Première of the film *Help* in 1965 and signed in ink around the neck by The Beatles, Cynthia Lennon and Brian Epstein, fetched £1,000/$1,600 in 1985, and a similar dress sold two years later for £4,000/$6,400.

A rare director's script for the film *A Hard Day's Night*, including the film script, signed on the title page by The Beatles, casting lists, call sheets, rates of pay and director's notes, was sold by the Second Assistant Director on the film for £3,500/$5,600 in 1987. At this sale at Phillips, a cardboard cut-out of a garden gnome, used on the front cover of the Sgt. Pepper album and signed by The Beatles on the front in a different colour for an assistant photographer during the shoot, sold for an astonishing £5,500/$8,800 over the telephone. Never before has so much interest been generated by a garden gnome!

The most avidly sought after autographs are handwritten letters, documents and lyrics. However, these are beyond most collectors' means, fetching upwards of £1,000/$1,600.

Don Short, a journalist who travelled with The Beatles between 1963 and 1970, sold a handwritten opening chapter of John Lennon's book *A Spaniard in the Works*, at a Phillips auction in 1987. He told me the story behind his acquisition of this important manuscript. 'Beatlemania was in full cry. We were hurtling through 1964 on a nationwide UK tour. Already John, Paul, George and Ringo were making headlines

Below A letter from Jimi Hendrix to a fan written during his first tour of the UK in 1967, when he was touring with Cat Stevens, Engleburt Humperdink, and The Walker Brothers.

Bottom John Lennon's handwritten lyrics for his song 'Imagine'. Sold for £5,800/$9,280 in 1988.

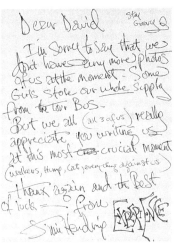

Right A cheque from John Lennon to the inland revenue. Sold for £4,800/$7,680 in 1988!

Below The Beatles' 'Please Please Me' album cover signed by all four, together with an autograph of Brian Epstein.

Please Please Me

THE BEATLES

PMC
1202

■ **GEORGE HARRISON** (lead guitar) ■ **JOHN LENNON** (rhythm guitar)
■ **PAUL McCARTNEY** (bass guitar) ■ **RINGO STARR** (drums)

SIDE ONE

1. I SAW HER STANDING THERE
   (McCartney-Lennon)
2. MISERY
   (McCartney-Lennon)
3. ANNA (GO TO HIM)
   (Alexander)
4. CHAINS
   (Goffin-King)
5. BOYS
   (Dixon-Farrell)
6. ASK ME WHY
   (McCartney-Lennon)
7. PLEASE PLEASE ME
   (McCartney-Lennon)

SIDE TWO

1. LOVE ME DO
   (McCartney-Lennon)
2. P.S. I LOVE YOU
   (McCartney-Lennon)
3. BABY IT'S YOU
   (David-Williams-Bacharach)
4. DO YOU WANT TO KNOW A SECRET
   (McCartney-Lennon)
5. A TASTE OF HONEY
   (Scott-Marlow)
6. THERE'S A PLACE
   (McCartney-Lennon)
7. TWIST AND SHOUT
   (Medley-Russell)

Recording first published 1963

TONY BARROW

USE
EMITEX
CLEANING MATERIAL

· E.M.I. RECORDS LIMITED
HAYES · MIDDLESEX · ENGLAND

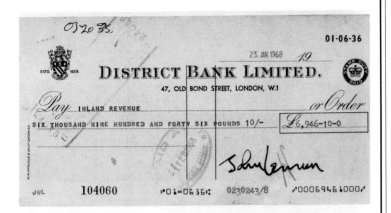

and I came to know them well as a newspaper columnist — in the process we became good friends. We checked into a country hotel somewhere between Birmingham and Leeds. After dinner John disappeared into the loo and emerged nearly an hour later clutching a torn white envelope and two brown disposal bags. He had scribbled notes all over them and at first I thought he intended showing me the lyrics of a new song he had written. Instead, he explained, it was the start of "a great new book". John thrust the pages into my hand after copying the text into a clean exercise book and said "Here Don. They're yours. Flog 'em if you ever go broke." It transpired that whilst John was in the toilet he had composed the first and title chapter of his second book *A Spaniard in the Works*. The manuscript sold for £11,000/ $17,600.

The following year, three original manuscript pages for the *Daily Howl* by John Lennon were sold for £12,000/$19,200. They were made up of textbook pages, covered with handwritten comic and nonsense poetry, prose and cartoon drawings. The *Daily Howl* formed the bases for both John Lennon's books.

A handwritten letter from Jimi Hendrix to a member of the Universal Autograph Collectors' Club, written in red ball point pen in 1967 when Hendrix was on his first British tour with Cat Stevens, The Walker Brothers and Engleburt Humperdink, — 'But we all (all 3 of us) really appreciate you writing us at this most crucial moment (Walkers, Hump, Cat and everything against us)' — sold at Phillips for £1,600/$2,560.

Rare handwritten lyrics for songs as famous as John Lennon's 'Imagine' and 'Jealous Guy', and Paul McCartney's 'She Came in Through the Bathroom Window' are in a class of their own. Pop collectors have to compete with investors and manuscript collectors to possess these jewels of rock memorabilia. In the mid-1980s, handwritten lyrics of this quality have been fetching between £7,000 and £15,000/ $11,200 and $24,000, so sadly many collectors can only dream of owning them.

Autograph collecting does have pitfalls. As prices soar, a

Below The original working script, call sheets and shooting schedule for the Beatles' film 'A Hard Day's Night' *c*.1964. Sold for £3,500/$5,600 in 1987.

Bottom A Rolling Stones fan club card, signed on the reverse by the group, including Brian Jones.

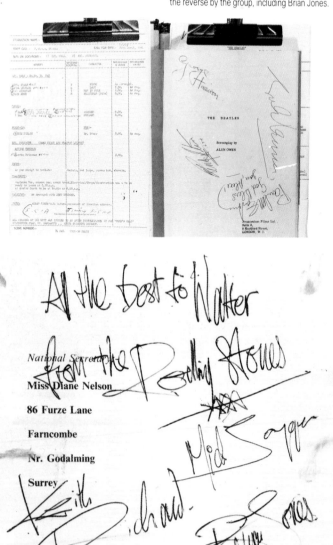

flood of fakes is appearing on the market. They may not just be recent counterfeits. It is well-known that at least ten people in The Beatles entourage, including roadies, secretaries and Mal Evans, regularly copied The Beatles' signatures for desperate fans. These autographs can be very good and in many cases are almost indistinguishable from authentic examples. It is only an experienced eye that can identify the false from an original. At Phillips, as many as two out of three Beatles' autographs brought in for valuation are not genuine. There are also a large number of facsimile or printed signatures on photographs and Official Beatles' Fan Club cards. They are easy to spot; if you examine one under a magnifying glass, you will notice there is no texture to the ink. Authentic Elvis Presley signatures are scarce. The words Elvis and Presley should always be linked together, but even this does not guarantee that they are authentic. It is best to examine the source of the signature to establish the likelihood of its being right. Two of the rarest signatures in the rock and pop file are those of Jim Morrison of The Doors and Jimi Hendrix. Both are now fetching over £300/$480, but, before spending this amount of money, always check them.

When you have been collecting for a number of years, you will find it easier to identify fake autographs. I would recommend joining The Universal Autograph Collectors' Club to receive regular news letters. The club organizes several fairs a year, with 20 to 30 stalls. Collectors meet up at these events, organize swops, buy and sell and catch up with the latest news. When buying an autograph from a dealer, ask for a certificate of autheniticity. Al

Below The garden gnome used on the front of the Beatles LP cover for 'Sgt Pepper's Lonely Hearts Club Band' signed by all four Beatles. Sold for £5,500/$8,800 in 1987.

Reuter, an important autograph and manuscript collector, advises that to be 100 per cent sure of an autograph being genuine, it is best to collect it in person from the artist either at the stage door or whenever you are lucky enough to bump into someone face to face. Even better, carry a camera and snap the artist signing your book, record or photograph. What better proof of authenticity can there be than being there yourself and recording it on film?

Chapter Three

STAGESTRUCK

Many fans dream of owning an item of clothing or jewellery that once belonged to Elvis Presley or one of The Beatles. Sometimes it is possible to purchase stage and screen clothing at auctions, but, sadly, as with all rare memorabilia, this clothing does not come cheap.

Many stage clothes are so elaborately crafted they have an instrinsic value even without their association with a famous person. A collection of spectacular bejewelled stage costumes belonging to Michael Jackson and The Jacksons came up for auction in London in 1988. Each costume was designed to sparkle and dazzle the audience. Sewn from exotic fabrics and decorated with diamanté, rhinestones and glass jewels, they caused a sensation when offered for auction. Michael Jackson's dazzling purple dance shoes, studded with hundreds of purple glass stones, sold for £4,000/$6,400. The red-printed and studded shirt and black satin diamanté trousers, worn, together with the shoes, on The Jacksons Live tour of 1981 and pictured on the cover of their album 'The Jacksons Live', sold for £4,400/$7,040. His brother Jackie's intricately embroidered stage costume of purple chiffon, gold thread, glass stones and diamanté was bought by a

costume museum for £1,200/$1,920.

Elvis Presley's clothing rarely comes up for auction and, when this happens, it is his stage clothing that is much in demand. His black suede jacket with a wide standing collar and red thong detail, worn at a concert in 1969, sold in London in 1985 for £4,950/$7,920. The jacket was sold by Larry Geller, Presley's private hairdresser. Elvis Presley's gold wristwatch, which he gave to a doctor who treated him for a dry sore throat in 1971, together with two prescriptions each signed by Elvis, sold for £6,820/$10,912 in 1986. Two years later, a diamond ring worn by Elvis in the mid-1970s sold to a Japanese collector for £3,000/$4,800, and a gold pendant with the monogram 'T.C.B.' Elvis's personal motto, 'Takin' Care of Business', and given by him to a friend, sold for £4,400/$7,040.

Stage and street clothes which formerly belonged to The Beatles have appeared in auctions in the US and the UK. The famous round-collared suits, worn by them in 1963 and made by the tailors D. A. Milling & Son, have been sold for between £1,800 and £4,000/$2,880 and $6,400 in the 1980s. Often the jacket will bear a Millings label on the inside pocket, and inside this the

Kim Wilde's black, turquoise, green and purple fluorescent stretch body suit, as worn on her video for the song 'The Second Time' *c.*1984.

Right Jackie Jackson's (of The Jackson Five) stage costume, pictured on the album 'The Jacksons Live' *c.* 1981.

Far right, top Michael Jackson's shirt, trousers and shoes as worn on 'The Jacksons Live' LP cover.

Far right, bottom Michael Jackson's dance shoes, each pair signed. Sold in 1988. The red pair fetching £1,800/$2,880 and the white satin pair fetching £3,800/$6,080.

Below Michael Jackson's purple, glass-studded dance shoes as worn by him on the cover of 'The Jacksons Live' album together with a signed note. Sold for £4,000/$6,400 in 1988.

lettered name of a Beatle and an order number. Paul McCartney's suit was sold with a note declaring 'Paul's thinner — take in waist and Paul says cloth is scratchy'! A silver lamé evening jacket worn by Ringo Starr when, as Richard Starkey, he was a member of the group Rory Storm and The Hurricanes and bearing his initials on the inside collar, was auctioned for £1,300/$2,080 in 1988. Clothes worn by John Lennon in the film *A Hard Day's Night* and a leather jacket he wore in the film *How I Won the War* both fetched well over £1,000/$1,600 in the mid-1980s. It is interesting to speculate on the price a collector would have to pay at auction for one of the original military style uniforms worn by The Beatles on the Sgt. Pepper's album front cover — if it was ever to appear!

Jimi Hendrix's clothing is very rare and when a colourful silk square he wore as a headband on stage came up for auction, it sold for £420/$672. In the same sale in 1987, a striped tuxedo jacket worn by Mick Jagger and donated by him to Kent Cricket Club, fetched £650/$1,040.

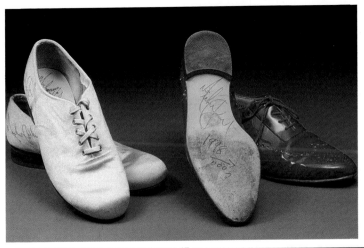

Perhaps the most striking stage costume to appear at auction in the late 1980s was sold by John Entwistle of The Who. The stage suit, tailored in red and yellow suede with a dramatic yellow flame motif, was worn by him when The Who appeared on Top of the Pops in the early 1970s. It sold for £1,300/$2,080, a high price for a collector to pay for an artist not yet as collectable as Elvis Presley or The Beatles, but it was a fine piece of 1970s nostalgia to acquire.

All the above-mentioned clothes were sold with good provenance. When buying clothes believed to have been owned by a celebrity, it is wise to ascertain their origin. If a document of authenticity is not available, a photograph of the artist wearing the costume is a good guarantee of original ownership. The difference in value of a jacket purported to have belonged to, rather than proven to have belonged to, an artist can be tenfold. If you possess an item but have no form of certification, it is worth following it up by searching for a photograph, a film clip or a letter that might confirm its provenance. In the past, the tailors D. A. Millings & Son have been able to supply letters verifying their Beatles' suits and these have subsequently been sold at auction. If the artist is still alive, there is a chance that he will be willing to certify that he wore the clothes. However, this type of inquiry rarely meets with a positive reply. Many artists of the 1960s and 1970s have become respectable pillars of society in the 1980s, and may not wish to be reminded of their youthful days of wearing psychedelic trousers and 'tinsel' platform shoes. Pop star and entertainer David Essex,

Boy George's peaked BOY hat, decorated by himself. Sold for £2,200/$3,520 in 1987.

on donating a flowery silk crêpe shirt to a charity auction, sent a note accompanying it with the words, 'Yes! Believe it or not, I did wear this shirt on various TV and concert performances in the seventies'. Many stars are not quite so forthcoming.

Charity auctions are a good source of clothing. Celebrities are approached directly to donate personal attire to the auction. Hence, there is little doubt that the items are genuine. At a charity auction at Phillips in 1987, on behalf of a drink- and drugs-related charity, Boy Goerge donated a remarkable hat which he had decorated himself with badges, safety pins and buttons. The hat, a BOY baseball cap, sold for £2,200/$3,520 to an American collector. At the same auction, a pair of designer gloves of zebra skin and leather, donated by Annie Lennox of The Eurythmics, sold for £550/$880. The high prices of stage clothes sold in the 1980s might be very discouraging to new collectors. However, many pop stars and entertainers of the 1980s regularly donate personal attire to charity auctions and this can often be bought for under £50/$80. Just as the stars of the 1970s have become collectable in the 1980s, the stars of today will be sought after in the 1990s.

Chapter Four

NOVELTIES

'Lot 224, A boxed set of "Bobb'n Head" Beatles' dolls selling to the gentleman on the right of the aisle for £400 [$640].' In the established old-school atmosphere of the London auction rooms, there was a gasp of astonishment and an air of disbelief that a collector could pay so much for what looked like a rather tacky set of plastic dolls. Five years later, with rock auctions an established part of the London salerooms, prices come as no surprise in this fast-growing field of collecting.

During the dizzy years of The Beatles' success, many people jumped on the bandwagon by manufacturing Beatles' souvenirs. Beatles' merchandise became big business and big bucks. In a vain attempt to keep control of items produced, Brian Epstein, The Beatles' manager, granted licences from The Beatles' company, Nems Enterprises. In America, licences were granted under the name of Seltaeb (Beatles spelt backwards). Many original items of merchandise carry the word '© Nems Ent. 1965' or 'm. by Seltaeb Inc.'. However, despite Epstein's efforts, hundreds of items were produced without this stamp of authority and are no less collectable.

The sale of The Beatles' merchandise was a phenomenon that has never been repeated and generated over $100 million in 1964 alone. One US manufacturer sold over two million T-shirts in a fortnight. In 1964, a Beatles' fan would eat, sleep and dream about The Beatles in a bedroom decorated with Beatles' wallpaper, Beatles' curtains, Beatles' pillows, sheets, bedcovers and blankets. Her daily routine would begin in a bath surrounded by the chirpy faces of John, Paul, George and Ringo on bathroom tiles, using Beatles' bubble-bath and talcum powder. She would wrap herself in a Beatles' towel and dress in Beatles underwear, Beatles' stockings and a cotton Beatles' dress. Her hair would be arranged with the help of Beatles' hairspray and around her neck would hang her Beatles' locket, on her wrist a Beatles' charm bracelet and on her clothes a variety of brooches. Her Beatles' school satchel would hold her Beatles' pencil case, ruler, wallet, keychain and diary, and her Beatles' lunchbox came complete with Beatles' thermos flask. When not listening to her many Beatles' singles, stored in a Beatles' record carrying case and sticking numerous cuttings into her Beatles' scrapbook, she would amuse herself and her equally Beatles-mad friends with her collection of Beatles' dolls,

Below A Corgi die-cast Yellow Submarine toy and a Beatles plastic guitar brooch.

Bottom An Irish Linen tea towel with printed picture of The Beatles.

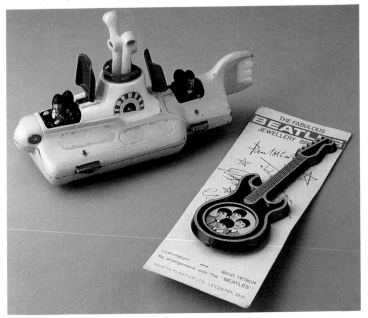

Beatles' cartoon kits, a 'Flip Your Wig' game, playing cards, a Beatles' magnetic hair game and, at Halloween, dress up in her special Beatles' Halloween costumes. She could drink her tea or coffee from a Beatles' pottery mug or cup and saucer, and eat her cereal at breakfast from pottery Beatles' bowls, on a Beatles' tablecloth. Her mother, on her birthday, would decorate her cake with tiny plastic Beatles' cake decorations. The list of merchandise available was endless.

Following the flood of items produced in 1964 and 1965, the number of licences was reduced. The next phase of merchandise followed the release of the film *The Yellow Submarine*, in which The Beatles were portrayed as cartoon characters. These cartoon figures were used on coathangers, stationery, candles, lunchboxes, watches and pop-up books. One of the most novel items was a yellow submarine die-cast toy made by Corgi Toys, complete with periscope and tiny plastic Beatles with movable

heads. In the late 1980s, this toy in its original box can fetch up to £100/$160. In addition to the *Yellow Submarine* merchandise, there are the original *Yellow Submarine* celluloids used in the film. These were sold in several New York Art Galleries in the early 1970s and were accompanied by a certificate of authenticity from Kings Features. Many spare celluloids found their way into dustbins and do not, therefore, have any provenance. They are difficult to handle at auction for, without sufficient proof of ownership, they are still regarded as the property of Subafilm, the makers of *Yellow Submarine* and, therefore, cannot be sold publicly. The most collectable celluloids are those featuring The Beatles cartoon figures or one of the other main characters, such as The Head Blue Meanie which sold for £300/$480, but a lady holding a bunch of flowers from the same film sold for only £100/$160.

The third phase of Beatles' merchandising arrived at the end of 1967, with the opening of the

A set of four Seltaeb plastic Beatle dolls with nylon hair and detachable musical instruments c.1964.

Apple boutique in Baker Street and the foundation of The Beatles' company Apple Corps Ltd. Apple novelties were produced for promotional purposes only and are, therefore, rare and highly collectable. The Apple Watch from Apple Corps Ltd., with a square face and an 'apple' dial, made by New England, can sell in its original box for £200/$320 in the mid-1980s. Another item seldom seen for sale is the Apple Dartboard with an 'apple' logo as its centre that was given to friends and employees of The Beatles. One sold in an auction in 1987 for £720/$1,152.

With so many different items of varying quality, it is difficult to know where to start collecting. An excellent guide to the merchandise produced is an American book entitled *Collecting The Beatles — An Introduction and Price Guide to Fab Four Collectables, Records and Memorabilia* by Barbara Fenick. Her price guide applies more to the American market, as rare items sold at auction in London tend to go well above her estimates. Below, I have listed The Beatles' merchandise that has appeared in sales in London in the mid- to late-1980s under five price guide categories.

Under £50/$80

A set of 60 A & BC bubblegum cards with black and white photographs with facsimile signatures
Washington pottery cereal bowls, plates, mugs, cups and saucers bearing portraits of The Beatles
A Worcester-ware tin tray bearing colourful Beatles' faces on a white background and red base
A set of plastic cake decorations
A Dorincourt ceramic tile of one of The Beatles or the group
A set of plastic Beatles' brooches
A pair of Ballito toffee-coloured nylons in original package
A Beatles 'wig'

£50-£100/$80-$160

A set of four glass tumblers with Beatles' faces on each and gold rim
An Irish linen tea towel, with maroon and white pictures of the Beatles
A Selcol 'New Sound' plastic guitar
Two coathangers made by

Right A Selcol 'New Sound' plastic Beatles guitar 58cm(23in) high.

Far right A pair of Beatles Sneakers, made by Wing Dings in the USA *c.* 1964 in original box.

Below A pair of Ballito Beatle stockings in original packing.

Right One from a set of four Beatle glass tumblers.

Far right A rare Dorincourt ceramic tile featuring The Beatles.

Saunders Ent. UK
A Corgi toy 'Yellow Submarine'
diecast toy in original box

£100-£200/$160-$320
Four plastic Beatles' 'strange
masks' in original packing
A 'With The Beatles' talc by
Margo of Mayfair
Three rolls of Beatles' wallpaper
A Beatles' blanket, cream with
printed faces, made by Witney
Blankets
A Beatles' bubblegum machine,
American *c*. 1965
A Beatles' bathmat
A Subutteo Beatles' miniature
figure set in original box
A pair of Beatles' sneakers
manufactured by Wing Ding, USA

£200-£300/$320-$480
A Selcol 'Ringo Starr New Beat
Drum' (without box)
A pair of Beatles' print curtains on
a yellow background
An Old England 'Apple' wrist
watch
A set of Seltaeb plastic Beatles'
dolls with nylon hair and musical
instruments
A set of 'Bobb'n Head' Beatles'
dolls manufactured by Car
Mascots Inc. USA, in original box
Candlewick bedcovers

Over £400/$640
A Beatles' cotton pink polka dot
dress
A Beatles' BEA flight bag
A Beatles' lampshade bearing
black and white Beatles' portraits
and song titles
An 'Apple' dartboard
A Beatles black vinyl carrying
case

There are a number of locations
to find Beatles merchandise.
Unfortunately, because of the high
prices realized at auctions, most
people are aware of the value of
Beatles-related items. This

Far right A Beatles plastic 'Kaboodle Kit' carrying
case, licensed by Nems Enterprises.

Below A gold metal Beatles brooch, 5cm(2in) high.

Far right A Beatles black vinyl carrying case, Nems
Enterprises Ltd, and leather metal Beatles belt.

publicity has had a good effect in that it has discovered many long forgotten items which are now being offered for sale. However, it has also encouraged people to believe that anything to do with The Beatles is very valuable, and many are disappointed with the low price their finds have realized at sale. It is still possible to find a bargain at jumble sales and bric-a-brac stalls. A number of Beatles' dresses have been found this way. Record collecting magazines, (see Chapter One) include sections where collectors and dealers advertise their wants and the items they wish to sell. In the UK, there is a week at the end of August each year when rock and pop and Beatles' collectors arrive to attend the rock and pop auctions and the Beatles Convention in Liverpool.

As in all the areas of collecting rock and pop memorabilia, there are counterfeits infiltrating the market. In the USA, a number of fakes have been found at Beatles' fairs and conventions being sold by unscrupulous dealers. The commonest counterfeits are The Beatles pen and desk sets, belts, ties and scarves. The TWA flight bag has also been reproduced. There is a collection of newly-made items bearing Beatles' decoration that never existed in the 1960s. Many of these have been made in Japan and Taiwan. A set of four Beatles' nodding dolls, stamped 'Made in Japan', came into Phillips, and the poor quality made me suspicious. An experienced eye can identify counterfeit items, but to a collector just starting out, caution is the keyword.

Although Beatles' merchandise and novelty items completely outnumber those produced for other artists, it is possible to gather quite a collection of

Below A Beatles bath mat.

novelties relating to Elvis Presley, The Rolling Stones, The Police and many other groups. A set of 1950s Elvis Presley pencils, still in their original package, sold at auction in 1987 for £130/$208. Colouring books, pillows, dog tags, hound dog soft toys, earrings and wallets have all appeared for sale, but in the mid-1980s, they are not as collectable as Beatles' merchandise. A set of 12 Rolling Stones' badges of an open mouth and tongue can fetch over £30/$48, and a set of 'Groovie Buttons' for The Jackson Five, promoting their hit song 'I'll Be There', sold for £25/$40 in 1987.

Bottom A set of Jackson Five Groovie buttons.

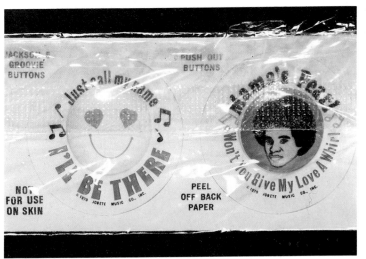

Chapter Five

PRECIOUS METAL

The glamorous side of the music industry is reflected in the awards presented to artists on the success of a record. Silver, gold and platinum presentation records are displayed in the homes of artists, in the offices of their management and in the boardroom and reception of their record companies.

The number of records an artist needs to sell to receive a silver, gold or platinum disc varies from country to country. The calculation may be based on the number of records sold or the amount of money generated. The discs themselves are made in a variety of different ways and few suppliers wish to divulge their technique. A few discs are known to have been coated with 24 carat gold, others are ordinary records that have been sprayed with gold car paint, and still others have been made up of metallic foil sandwiched between two clear sheets of vinyl.

Each official disc is accompanied by a B.P.I. plaque or, in the US, an R.I.A.A. plaque, bearing details of to whom the plaque is presented and the number of sales. For each successful record, the record company orders a gold disc for the artist, the band, management and record company staff. Those presented to the artist may not be unique, as he can, if he wishes, order five or six identical discs for his family and friends. Discs presented to record companies may be produced in fairly large numbers and their collectable value lies in their decorative quality and not their rarity. Most discs of this nature can be bought at auction for between £100 and £300/$160 and $480.

Certain gold discs have sold for very high prices. One presented to The Beatles can fetch far more than £1,000/$1,600, and records presented to artists who have since died are also sought-after. A gold disc for the Sgt. Pepper's Lonely Hearts Club Band, presented to The Beatles, sold to a collector in 1984 for £14,000/$22,880. A gold 78 rpm disc presented to Gene Vincent, for his song 'Be Bopa Lula' in 1956, sold for £9,000/$4,400. Discs presented to Jimi Hendrix, John Lennon, Bob Marley, Brian Jones, Marc Bolan and Keith Moon are likely to fetch four figures if offered for sale.

Presentation records from the 1980s have been fetching surprisingly high prices. A platinum disc presented to Paul Young in 1986, for his record 'Between Two Fires', sold for £8,090/$12,944, and a gold disc presented to Simon Le Bon, for Duran Duran's album 'Notorious',

A presentation gold 78rpm disc presented to Gene Vincent for his song 'Be Bop A Lula'. Sold in 1987 for £9,000/$14,400.

fetched £800/$1,280 in 1987.

One of the most enthusiastic collectors of gold discs in the 1980s has been The Hard Rock Café. The walls of the restaurants in London, New York, Dallas and Los Angeles are covered with shiny gold and silver discs, including ones presented to The Beatles, Jimi Hendrix, Blondie, Fleetwood Mac and The Beach Boys.

With the high prices being realized at auction, unscrupulous dealers in the UK and the US have been faking presentation discs, even to the extent of reproducing

A signed album cover for The Beatles 'Let It Be' LP mounted beside a display 'souvenir' gold disc.

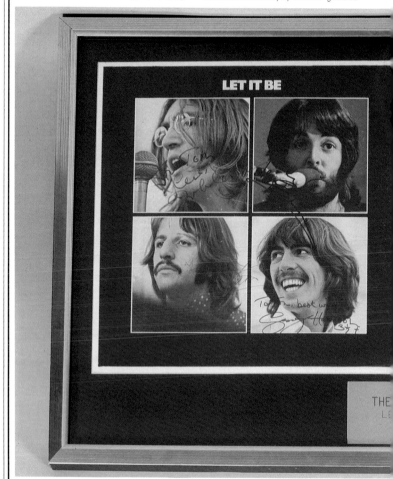

the official B.P.I. or R.I.A.A. plaques. The only foolproof way of knowing whether a disc is an original is to take it direct to the B.P.I. or one of their main suppliers who will examine it and provide a letter of authenticity.

Souvenir gold discs have been produced in large quantities in the USA where collectors choose to use them as decorative displays, often mounting them together with a set of autographs or a signed record cover. A Beatles' 'Let It Be' souvenir disc mounted beside the signed album sold in an auction in 1987 for

£1,300/$2,080, the value being in the rare signed album rather than the disc.

Records are not the only form of award presented to artists. A number of certificates have appeared in sales, including a set of ten Citations of Achievement presented to John Lennon by the Broadcast Music Inc. in 1964, each one representing one million airplays on US radio. They included the songs 'A Hard Day's Night', 'She's A Woman', and 'I Feel Fine', and sold at auction for between £250 and £700/$400 and $1,120. A Golden Octave Award

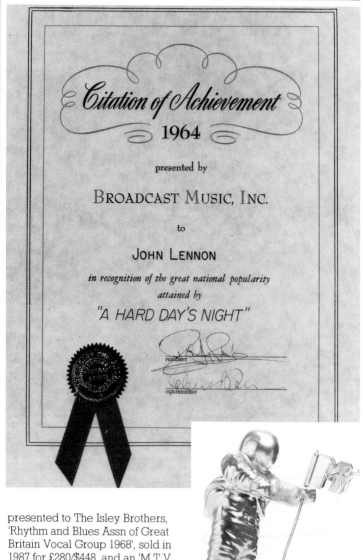

Citation of Achievement

1964

presented by

BROADCAST MUSIC, INC.

to

JOHN LENNON

in recognition of the great national popularity
attained by

"A HARD DAY'S NIGHT"

PRESIDENT

VICE-PRESIDENT

VIDEO MUSIC AWARD
1985–1986
JACK BONNI
BEST VIDEO OF THE YEAR
MONEY FOR NOTHING

presented to The Isley Brothers, 'Rhythm and Blues Assn of Great Britain Vocal Group 1968', sold in 1987 for £280/$448, and an 'M.T.V. Man on the Moon Video Music Award' for Dire Straits 'Best Video of the Year' for 'Money for Nothing' sold at a charity sale for £380/$608. Charity sales are the best source of presentation records, certificates and awards, many of which are donated directly by the artist and accompanied by a letter of authenticity.

Left A Citation of Achievement 1964 presented to John Lennon in recognition of the great national popularity attained by 'A Hard Day's Night', Broadcast Music Inc.

Bottom left An MTV Video Music Award 'Man on the Moon' presented for Dire Straits' promotional video 'Money for Nothing'.

Below A BPI presentation gold disc for Billy Idol's LP 'Whiplash Smile' *c.* 1968.

Chapter Six

ON TOUR

Most rock and pop fans have attended a live concert and taken home a tour programme, T-shirt, badge, ticket stub, poster or promotional tour jacket. Many of these ephemeral pieces are now fetching high prices in sales of rock memorabilia.

Concert posters, in particular, are becoming collectors' items, with rare examples fetching high figures when offered for sale. One of the historically most important posters to appear for sale in the 1980s was a hand-painted poster advertising the appearance of The Beatles and Rory Storm and The Hurricanes at the Kaiserkeller Club, Hamburg, 1960. This poster sold for £1,000/$1,600 in 1984. It seemed an astonishing price to pay for such an item then, but the poster has quadrupled in value by 1988. Any early poster for a Beatles' concert appearance is rare. Their 1964 Christmas Show, concert poster, sold together with three of the concert programmes for £1,650/$2,640. Another poster, advertising a Joe Brown concert in 1962 with an appearance by The Beatles and signed by Paul McCartney, sold for £2,530/$4,048.

The Beatles are not the only band that commands high prices for their concert posters. A rare poster for The Who's appearance at the Marquee Club in 1964 sold to a collector for £2,090/$3,344. The most sought-after posters date from the 1950s and 60s, but a decorative poster as recent as 1986 can be collectable if it is rare. In 1988, a poster for a concert billing The Who, Humble Pie, Lou Reed and Bad Company appearing at Charlton Athletic Football Club in 1974, and designed by Kosh, sold for £140/$224. A set of four posters for Generation X appearing at the Marquee Club in the late 1970s sold for £190/$304 and a concert

A selection of 1960s tour programmes.

poster for Siouxsie and The Banshees' North American Tour of 1986 sold for £75/$120. All Sex Pistols' material is rare and a concert poster for their last UK tour of 1977, 'Never Mind The Bans', sold for £340/$544. A poster advertising a concert played outside the US or the UK will be rarer and valuable. This was demonstrated when a poster for Cliff Richard's Russian tour sold for £420/$672.

Early tour programmes, particularly those dating from the 1950s and 60s, have become collectable. Most can still be purchased for under £50/$80 and are, therefore, available to most collectors. These programmes provide a fascinating insight into how concerts were arranged, the types of artists billed together and the theatres they played at (many of which have since closed down). The advertisements within the programmes give us an idea of the fashions and merchandise available to fans during the 1950s and 1960s. The order of billing is

also interesting to follow as groups became more or less popular.

Most sought-after are the tour programmes for The Beatles' early concerts when they appeared as the bottom billing! On their first UK nationwide tour, they appeared bottom of a six-act bill, headed by a 16-year-old girl, Helen Shapiro , voted 'Best Female Singer' in 1961. On the final night of the tour, The Beatles were elevated from the warm-up spot to the last act in the first half. Following this tour, The Beatles

A concert poster for The Who and friends designed by Kosh c.1974.

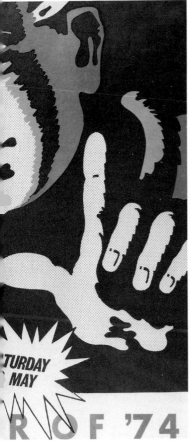

joined American artists Tommy Roe and Chris Montez and, by audience demand, were promoted from third act to top act, playing the all-important closing spot. Between May and June 1963, The Beatles toured with Roy Orbison, who began as top attraction but was soon relegated to second place. Within a week of the tour's commencement, the cover of the souvenir tour programme had to be reprinted, changing the name of the star billing from Roy Orbison to The Beatles. The Beatles' tour programmes for their tour to Paris, where they appeared with Trini Lopez and Sylvie Vartan, and for their Australian Tour of 1964 are both sought-after, together with the programme for The Beatles' concert at Carnegie Hall, New York in February 1964.

As these programmes have become collectable, more have begun to appear in auctions in job lots of four or five. In 1987, six souvenir programmes, including tours by Buddy Holly and The

Crickets, Johnnie Ray, The Teenagers with Frankie Lyman and The Platters (c.1956/57) sold for £240/$384. A collection of five 1960s programmes, including Gerry & The Pacemakers, Adam Faith, Gene Vincent and R'n'B 64, sold for £220/$352, and a rare 1964 Australian Tour Programme for The Beatles, sold with an original ticket for the concert at Sydney Stadium, realized £150/$240 in 1988. When a concert is cancelled after the programmes have been printed they become collectors'
items. A Wings' concert programme for their cancelled tour of Japan in 1980 can fetch £50/$80.

When buying a programme, it is worth checking through the pages as an original ticket or backstage pass is often still tucked inside. It is not unusual to buy a tour programme and find later that it bears several signatures of artists inside.

Often when fans attend concerts, they buy promotional T-shirts. They are worn with such

Left A Sex Pistols Promotional T. Shirt given away free with the Sex Pistols Press kit.

Above The Jacksons 'World Tour 1979' oyster satin tour jacket.

Right A Sex Pistols 'Never Mind The Bans' concert poster 1977 advertising their last UK tour.

Below The Rolling Stones Concert Poster for their US tour 1975 appearing at The Cow Palace, San Francisco. The poster was designed by Alton Kelly and Stanley Mouse.

enthusiasm that few survive in good condition. When they do appear for sale, they can fetch upwards of £30/$48. A Michael Jackson 'Victory Tour 1984' T-shirt sold at auction in 1988 for £130/$208 and a Sex Pistols' 'Never Mind The Bollocks' handpainted T-shirt sold for £200/$320. Beware when buying Beatles' T-shirts, as many of the original 1960s shirts have been reproduced.

Tour jackets are growing in popularity, as artists' personal clothing becomes too highly priced for most collectors. The majority of tour jackets offered for sale can be bought for under £250/$400, and collectors who buy them often wear them on a day-to-day basis. They are a practical buy and an investment. The most sought-after jackets are those worn by a member of a

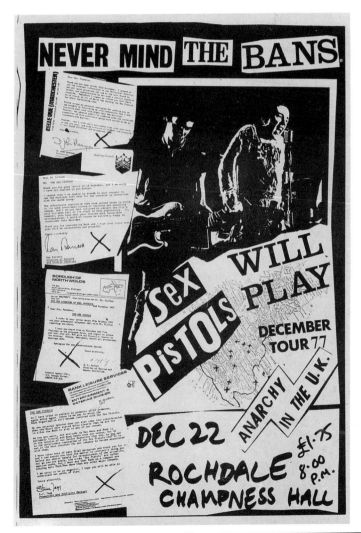

Siouxsie and The Banshees promotional poster.

band and bearing his name
embroidered on the front. On a
tour, the management would have
20 or so jackets made for the
band, roadies, management,
wives and girlfriends. The record
company would have as many as
100 made for promotion, and
another 500 might be sold as
merchandise. American collector,
Bo Overlock, in his own words 'a
compulsive collector', who has
over 20 different tour jackets in his
collection of rock memorabilia
says 'it is only a very experienced
eye that can tell whether a tour
jacket was made for the band, the
record company or as
merchandise'. He usually
identifies the jacket by its quality.
His favourite tour jacket is for 'The
Who in Europe 1975', one of only
25 made. Early tour jackets were
made of satin, followed by
baseball jackets and more
recently leather jackets, which no
doubt will be expensive to collect
in the future. The more obscure
the tour, the more collectable the
tour jackets. A jacket for Queen's
South American, Australian or
Japanese tour would be much
more collectable than a jacket
from an American or UK tour. No
tour jackets were made for any of
The Beatles' tours and those
circulating at record and Beatles'
conventions are fakes.

Chapter Seven

KALEIDOSCOPE EYES

A small collection of psychedelic posters has started to appear in specialized sales of rock and pop memorabilia. Designed and produced between 1967 and 1969, they were forgotten for 20 years, only to reappear, selling for surprising prices in the auction rooms in the late 1980s. Little is known about the history of these decorative posters, the designers and how many were produced. As prices have soared in recent years, so more posters have started to appear. Reprints have infiltrated the market and many inexperienced collectors have been deceived by them.

The majority of psychedelic posters were printed in 1967. This was the year of 'Sgt. Pepper's Lonely Hearts Club Band', the campaign to legalize cannabis, the opening of the Apple Boutique in Baker Street and the emergence of a number of subversive underground magazines including *IT — The International Times* and *Oz* magazine and the notorious *Oz 'School Kids Issue'* and subsequent trial.

A design team, which captured the flavour of 1967, was 'The Fool'. It comprised three Dutch artists, Simon Posthuma, Josje Leeger and Marijke Koger, who had been commissioned to design a logo for the Sgt. Pepper album cover.

They were also responsible for the repainting of John Lennon's Rolls Royce in wild psychedelic colours. Following this success, The Beatles commissioned them to design a series of clothes and posters for their forthcoming boutique which opened as The Apple Boutique in December 1967. They went as far as incorporating their wild designs on to walls, ceilings, cash-tills and furniture. They painted a giant mural, 20 yards/18 metres high on the outside of the building to the amazement (and to some, horror) of the public. Posters designed by 'The Fool' are now fetching over £100/$160 at auction.

Hapsash and The Coloured Coat, the two-man design team of Nigel Weymouth and Michael English, produced some of the most decorative and now sought-after posters of the period. During the years 1967 to 1969, Hapsash and The Coloured Coat designed over 20 concert posters and one film poster. Their most collectable posters are those designed for the underground clubs, The U.F.O. Club (believed to stand for 'Underground Freak Out!') and the Middle Earth Club. In the mid-1980s, these posters were fetching over £400/$640.

The year 1967, when youth was 'wild and free', saw the emergence of a number of avante

Martin Sharp's 'Jimi Hendrix Explosion' poster. This illustration first appeared in *Oz* magazine and was subsequently published as a poster by The Big O Poster Co.

Below right An American kaleidoscope circular poster promoting concerts with Jefferson Airplane, Flaming Grooves, Canned Heat, Grateful Dead *c.*1967

Right A collection of Peter Max psychedelic le, inflatable plastic cushions and holdall.

Below A psychedelic poster designed by Hapsash and The Coloured Coat for the Middle Earth club advertising forthcoming gigs.

garde and subversive magazines. *Oz* magazine ran a brother company called The Big O (OZ) Poster Co, and designers worked on both the magazines and the posters. The most notable of these was an Australian designer, Martin Sharp, whose striking psychedelic designs are now familiar in the auction rooms. One of his first poster designs, entitled 'Jimi Hendrix Explosion', originated as a design in Issue 15 of *Oz*. Other popular Martin Sharp posters are Bob Dylan's 'Blowing in the Wind' silk-screen printed on to metallic paper and the 'Legalise cannibis' poster, silk-screen printed on to a gold metallic background and designed for the Legalise Cannabis Rally held in Hyde Park on 16 July, 1967.

A series of psychedelic posters familiar to collectors of Beatles' memorabilia is the set of four Richard Avedon posters produced in a limited edition by the *Daily Express*. John, Paul, George and Ringo were photographed in varying psychedelic tones and the set, framed and displayed, has sold regularly for £500/$800 at auction in the 1980s.

A number of American designers were producing very decorative posters at the same time. Artists Rick Griffin, Stanley Mouse, Alton Kelly and Peter Max produced many concert posters. Peter Max, who ran his own design company, diversified into furniture and a colourful set of plastic cushions, each bearing an individual design, sold for £110/$176 at Phillips in 1988. A concert poster for the Rolling Stones' US tour, when they appeared at The Cow Palace, San Francisco, designed by Alton Kelly and Stanley Mouse, sold for £150/$240 in the same sale.

Below A green and turquoise psychedelic display, with 'mirrored' glasses.

Right 'A is for Apple' psychedelic poster designed by 'The Fool'.

Right A collection of 1960s psychedelic and underground magazines.

Bottom right Pink Floyd at the UFO Club psychedelic poster designed by Hapsash and The Coloured Coat and re-printed by the Chelsea Publishing Co in the early 1970s.

Below Peter Max LOVE poster.

The relatively new field of collecting and surprisingly high prices realized at auction for psychedelic posters has resulted in a number of lower quality posters and reprints appearing on the market. Some collectors with insufficient knowledge have been handling these posters and reprints in the belief that they were 1960s originals. A few Hapsash and the Coloured Coat posters have been reprinted, but no reprints of Martin Sharp's work have been found.

Little has been written on the subject, but there are a few basic guidelines to follow in order to avoid handling reprints.

a) Original posters by Hapsash and The Coloured Coat and Martin Sharp were silk-screen printed.
b) Each poster should have the name of The Big O Poster Co or Osiris Visions or Agency on the side or bottom of the poster.
c) The majority of the posters measured 20 by 30 inches/51 by 76 cm.

Osiris Visions went into liquidation in 1969 and, for a brief period, was taken over by The Chelsea Publishing Co, which reprinted several of the more decorative posters in the early 1970s. These early reprints are still collectable but do not command such high prices as their silk-screen originals.

Some of the more commercial designs of 1967 have been reprinted by fans in the early 1980s. These include the posters for the concerts 'The Stones and Frank Zappa', 'The Magical Mystery Tour', 'The Sgt. Pepper's Lonely Hearts Club Band' and 'The Stones in the Park', which was originally named 'Tomorrow My White Bicycle!'.

Legalise Cannabis poster designed by Martin Sharp and advertising the Legalise Pot Rally, July 1967.

A set of Richard Avedon psychedelic portraits of The Beatles *c.*1967. These posters were originally available by mail order through the Daily Express newspaper for thirty-six shillings.

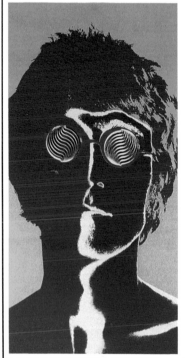

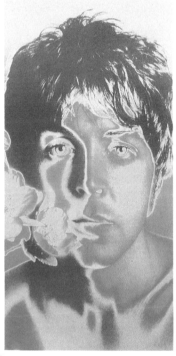

Many American posters for the San Francisco concerts at the Avalon and Fillmore ballrooms have been reprinted in the UK in large numbers. These are easily identified, as they bear the printed words 'San Francisco Poster Co.'. Although of little value, these reprints are often bought by collectors who cannot afford to pay the higher prices of the original 1960s edition but who wish to keep a record of the design.

An American poster promoting The First Annual Love Circus at Winterland, designed by Herrick c.1967.

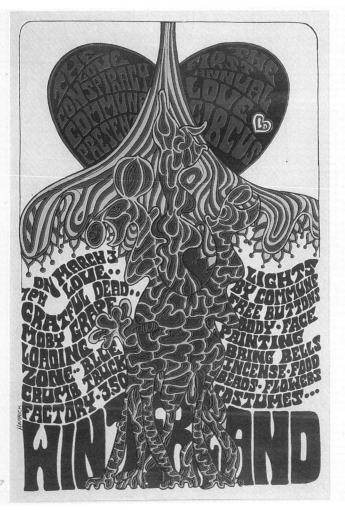

Chapter Eight

MUSEUM PIECES

The most important items offered for sale in recent years are the musical instruments artists have played and on which they have composed their songs. Some unique musical instruments have appeared at auctions and been purchased by private collectors, museums and The Hard Rock Café. This is the one field of collecting when condition is not the over-riding factor. The more 'used' the guitar, the more attractive it is to collectors. Pete Townshend's Rickenbakker guitar, which he joyfully smashed to pieces on Top of the Pops in 1966, sold recently for £3,000/$4,800.

If you are offered the opportunity to buy an item of this nature, only consider it if the instrument is accompanied by a certificate or letter of authenticity and, if possible, a photograph of the artist playing it. Prices for this rare memorabilia are high and the only way for an enthusiastic collector with limited means to acquire such an instrument, save by mortgaging his house, would be to win it at a charity raffle. John Bonham of Led Zeppelin donated his Ludwig drum kit as a raffle prize to a charity ball on behalf of his local children's home. It was resold ten years later in 1988 for £3,000/$4,800.

Many instruments generously donated by artists for charity have been resold later for very high prices. For this reason, artists are becoming cautious about donating items of memorabilia and are more likely to offer limited edition posters, books and records than musical instruments and personal clothing.

At charity auctions, it is advisable to read the catalogue description of each lot carefully. An instrument may have been donated by an artist, but this does not mean he has played it. Often artists, who are besieged daily by charities asking them to donate a personal memento, will instruct a secretary or manager to buy a guitar which they then sign. These instruments are still collectable and always realize a good price for the charity. A 'Heritage' guitar, donated by Eric Clapton and signed by him on the body, was sold in a charity auction in 1987 for £2,800/$4,480.

Detailed below are the most important and interesting musical instruments to appear at auction in London and the price they realized. It is interesting to note the way the market has moved, which artists are commanding the high prices and the amount collectors are prepared to pay for a unique instrument.

Errol Brown of Hot Chocolate's Yamaha 6 string, acoustic guitar with the song titles he composed on this guitar etched on to the front, including 'Emma', 'You Sexy Thing' and 'Brother Louie'.

John Bonham's Ludwig drum set originally
donated by John Bonham to a charity ball in 1979
and sold at auction in 1988 for £3,000/$4,800.

The most important musical instruments to appear at auction in London in the 1980s

1981
George Harrison's 12-string Harptone guitar Model L/12NC Serial No 2004/27 used by George for several years
Sold for £3,000/$4,800

Paul McCartney's Chappell & Co Ltd. upright piano No. 38567 in ebonized case
Sold for £9,000/$14,400

John Lennon's Steinway upright piano
Sold for £7,500/$12,000

1982
Paul McCartney' drum kit with a letter from Mike McCartney and a photograph of Paul playing the drums
Sold for £2,320/$3,712

An Audiotek/Cadec mixing console used by John Lennon to record the Imagine album and installed in Lennon's private studio
Sold for £6,050/$9,680

1983
Marc Bolan's polished aluminium electric guitar, custom-made for him in America and inscribed Marc Bolan J.V., with a stylish flying head mounted with a red cut stone
Sold for £2,310/$3,696

John Lennon's Phantom Vox electric guitar organ with a letter of authenticity signed by George Harrison
Sold for £8,800/$14,080

John Lennon's Broadwood upright piano with ebonized case, gilt lining, candle holders and brass plaque 'On this piano was written A Day In the Life, Lucy in the Sky

with Diamonds, Good Morning, Good Morning and others, John Lennon 1971'
Sold for £8,800/$14,080

1984
Bill Wyman's Framus 'Star bass' bass guitar
Sold for £3,080/$4,928

Brian Jones's Vox electric six-string guitar with a signed photograph of Brian Jones using it
Sold for £3,520/$5,632

Elton John's painted upright piano
Sold for £2,200/$3,520

George Harrison's six-string Harptone Acoustic guitar with letter of authenticity from Harold J. Harrison
Sold for £4,070/$6,512

The original painted bass drum skin for The Beatles, marked Ludwig. 'The Beatles' handpainted in black
Sold for £4,620/$7,392

John Lennon's Hofner Compensator steel string acoustic guitar with a letter of authenticity by George Harrison saying 'the Hofner is one of the first guitars of John's going back to the early days in Liverpool'
Sold for £17,050/$27,280

1985
Jimi Hendrix's Gibson SC Type 2 Custom Guitar *c.*1969
Sold for £7,700/$12,320

Ginger Baker's Ludwig drum set
Sold for £39,760/$63,616

Keith Moon's drums dating from 1969 to 1975
Sold for £5,280/$8,448

1986
Bill Haley's Aria PE 180 electric semi-acoustic guitar with a Bill Haley play list attached to it with tape and played by him on British and South African tours
Sold for £15,500/$24,800

A set of Reindeer bells with red wooden handles used by John Lennon for the recording of 'Happy Christmas (War is Over)' in 1972
Sold for £900/$1,440

John Lennon's Vox Amplifier used by Lennon in the Pop Poll Awards 1963
Sold for £2,530/$4,048

Stuart Sutcliffe's Hofner 'President' Base guitar which he bought at a Liverpool Music Shop in 1960
Sold for £10,450/$16,720

1987
Errol Brown's (of Hot Chocolate) Yamaha six-string acoustic guitar with songs 'You Sexy Thing', 'Emma' and 'Brother Louie' engraved on front
Sold for £1,200/$1920

A Piccolo Octave Trumpet used to record the solo trumpet part in The Beatles song 'Penny Lane' and on the recording of 'All You Need is Love'
Sold for £5,800/$9,280

1988
John Entwistle's Peter Cook Customized Fender Electric bass guitar, finished in orange and red flame design, used by Entwistle on The Who's appearance on Top of The Pops in the early 1970s
Sold for £15,000/$24,000

John Bonham's Ludwig drum set, originally donated to a charity raffle
Sold for £3,000/$4,800

Chapter Nine

USEFUL ADDRESSES

Listed below are a number of addresses of museums, fan clubs, information services, and magazines that will be of interest to collectors of Rock and Pop Memorabilia.

Where to see items on display:

Theatre Museum
Russell Street
Covent Garden
LONDON WC2

Hours of opening: Tuesday to Friday 11am to 7pm

The museum has a growing rock and pop section devoted to stage and screen clothing and ephemera. Major items include The Beatles stage suits, Keith Moon's drums and jump suit. Mick Jagger's jump suit, Pete Townsend's smashed guitar and stage clothing belonging to Marc Bolan, Gary Glitter, Adam Ant and many others.

Madame Tussauds
Marylebone Road
LONDON NW1 5LR

Among the many waxworks on display are Michael Jackson, David Bowie, The Beatles, Grace Jones, Elvis Presley and Bob Geldof.

Jimmy Velvet's Elvis Presley Museum
110 Poplar Street
Franklin
Tennessee 37064
USA

Gracelands
PO Box 16508
Memphis
Tenessee 38186
USA

Fan Clubs and information services:

Elvis Presley Fan Club of Great Britain
PO Box 4
Leicester
Leicestershire
England

Beatles Fan Club of Great Britain
Superstore Productions
123 Marina
St Leonards on Sea
East Sussex
TN38 0BN

Beatles Unlimited (Dutch fan club)
c/o Rene Van Haarlem
PO Box 602
3430 ap nieuwegein
Netherlands

Jimi Hendrix Information
Management Institute
Box 374
Des Plaines
Illinois 60016
USA

Universal Autograph Collectors
Club
PO Box 467
Rockville Centre
NY 11571
USA

Marc Bolan Official Fan Club
PO Box 10
Bath
Avon
BA1 1YH
England

David Bowie
Bowie Friends
119 Queens Crescent
London NW5
England

Phil Collins
PO Box 107
London N6 5RU
England

Culture Club
PO Box 40
Ruislip HA4 7ND
England

Duran Duran
PO Box 179
Birmingham B1 2DL
England

Genesis
PO Box 107
London N6 5RU
England

The Jacksons
PO Box 9488
North Hollywood
California 91609
USA

Michael Jackson
EMMC
7635 Fulton Avenue
North Hollywood
California 91605
USA

The World of Michael Jackson
PO Box 1804
Encino
California 91426-1804
USA

National Kiss HQ
6430 Variel Avenue
102 Woodland Hills
California 91367
USA

Wings Fan Club
PO Box 4UP
London W1A 4UP
England

Pink Floyd
Cedarstraat 3B
3203 BA
Spkenisse
Holland

The Police
Outlandos Fan Club
194 Kensington Park Road
London W11
England

Rolling Stones Official Fan Club
PO Box 200
Surbiton
Surrey KT6 4NH
England

Siouxsie and The Banshees
Bravado
71B Gowan Avenue
Fulham
London SW6
England

The Who Club
PO Box 107A
London N6 5RU
England

Magazines

Record Collector
43-45 St Mary's Road
Ealing
London W5 5RQ
England

Goldmine
Krause Publications Inc
Iola
WI 54990
USA

Good Day Sunshine – Beatles fan
publication
Liverpool Productions
397 Edgewood Avenue
New Haven
CT 06511
USA

Beatles Unlimited – Fan Club
bi-monthly magazine
PO Box 602
3430 ap niewegein
Netherlands

TO ANGUS AND ALEXANDER

Acknowledgements

I would like to thank Al Reuter, Joe
Long, Bo Overlock, Warwick
Stone, Isacc Tigrett, my assistant
Andrew Milton and my director
Andrew Hilton for their continued
help and support of Phillips' Sales
of Rock and Pop Memorabilia.